little book of
Kalm

KIM JONG-UN'S
little book of
Kalm

SB

Published in the UK in 2019 by Short Books
Unit 316, ScreenWorks,
22 Highbury Grove, London N5 2ER

10 9 8 7 6 5 4 3 2 1

A CIP catalogue record for this book is available
from the British Library.

ISBN 978-1-78072-406-5

Printed and bound in Great Britain by
CPI Group (UK) Ltd, Croydon, CR0 4YY

Page Layouts by Short Books

A little note from your self-help guru, the Shining Sun, Great Successor, Brilliant Comrade and the Supreme Leader of the Democratic People's Republic of Korea:

As the world's youngest head of state, life can be difficult and stressful. Fortunately for me – and for you reading this – I am also the world's most intelligent person and a genius at keeping *kalm*.

The day I was born a double rainbow suddenly appeared in the sky and blessed me with the awe-inspiring power of *karefree koolness*. From this moment on I was gifted a miraculous self-care regime which has enabled me to step back, slow down and stay on the smooth path to inner peace – no matter what is going on around me.

Within these pages I give to you, my people, the best tips from my relaxation toolkit. I know you'll find this ESSENTIAL reading and you will follow my advice CORRECTLY – this is the first lesson you must learn: balance and *kalm* is about discipline. Read on to find out other ways to quieten your mind, make sense of the chaos and be happy.

Keep kalm,

Kim

A mantra for joy

Repeat this mantra to calm a stressful mind:
Smiling brings me joy, laughter lightens my load.

Express yourself

Hiding your opinions, denying your needs and suppressing your emotions leads to inner stress and unhappiness. Let it all out!

Contemplate nature

Nature is healing. Schedule some breaks into your day to soak up all that nature has to offer.

A breathing exercise

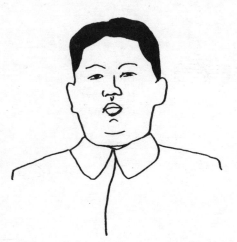

Stand in front of the mirror, breathe deeply, look at yourself admiringly. Do this for 15 minutes every day.

Detox

KILLER KALE SMOOTHIE

1 cup kale
1 cup spinach
1/2 avocado
1 cup almond milk
1 drop VX*
Sprinkle of flax seeds

*available at select local pharmacies

This delicious smoothie is full of punchy potassium for an electrifying kick. Just pop all the ingredients into a nutribullet and blitz together, then serve to friends and family for breathtaking results!

A mindful practice:
the big red button

- Sit down on a chair in front of the red button and place your finger lightly on the button.

- Now, with this button under your finger, you can begin to explore it with all of your senses.

- Focus on the button as if you've never seen anything like it before. Scan it, exploring every part of it, focus on really seeing the essence of this button.

- Notice where the surface reflects light or becomes darker.

- Next, explore the texture, feeling the hardness and smoothness of the button.

- While you're doing this, if thoughts arise such as "Why am I doing this weird exercise?" or "How will this ever help me?" then see if you can acknowledge these thoughts, let them be, and then bring your awareness back to the button.

- Lean over the button until your nose is just above it and carefully notice the smell of it.

- Now, return your finger to the button and circle it, consider pressing the button and what this might feel like. But resist actually pressing the button.

- Take a moment to congratulate yourself for taking this time to experience mindfully not pressing the button – today at least.

Gentle exercise

Go for a soulful walk in a green space to slow down any racing thoughts.

Appreciate your loved ones

Don't be complacent about the love you share with others. Keep your friends close, and your family closer.

"I never came upon any of my discoveries through the process of rational thinking."

Albert Einstein

A meditation exercise

Imagine you are the sun. The world revolves around you. People bask in your warmth. Your presence affects every living thing. You are the most important being in the universe. Harness these thoughts.

Retail therapy

Sometimes a trip to the shops is the easiest method of distraction.

A new perspective

Try to look at your life from a distance while staying neutral and detached.

Say goodbye to the toxic people in your life

Who you spend time with is who you become. So, choose carefully. Surround yourself with "right thinking" people.

Dress kool

Revamp your style for an easy feel-good fix.

Group exercise

Working out with other health-minded gym-goers can be a powerful motivation and help influence your mood for the better.

Take time to stop

Invest time in YOU. When we forget to check whether we are doing okay, we can't be at our best.

Gratitude

It is important to know not just how to thank others but also how to receive thanks. Write a list of all those who owe you some gratitude. Then decide how exactly they should show their appreciation.

"Who says you're not perfect?
Who says you're not beautiful?
Who says?"

Selena Gomez

Choose your friends wisely

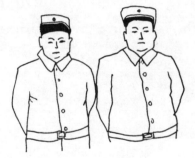

Surround yourself with physically strong people,
to ward off pestering imperialists.

Keeping busy

Create a project to keep yourself occupied and to give your mind a break from anxious thoughts.

The authentic you

Strive to find your authentic voice. Connect to who you truly are in order to live in harmony with who you desire to become.

Technology detox

Spending too much time on your phone can increase stress levels significantly. Take a break from the noise with a technology detox.

Positive affirmations

Try saying this positive affirmation at the beginning of each day to feel empowered and fabulous: *I am a great person.*

Your body is your temple

Make sure your body is cleansed with the most nutritious food. Always listen to your gut.

A sleeping remedy

Something keeping you up at night? Unwind by counting army personnel in your head.

Hobbies for relaxation

Manual labour is a balm for the soul and an antidote to the noise of modern life.

"What lies behind us and what lies before us are tiny matters compared to what lies within us."

Ralph Waldo Emerson

Zones of safety

Create a safe place you can retreat to when times get tough.

How to make new friends

Look out for someone who will show a genuine interest in what's going on in your life, what you have to say, and how you think and feel. And most importantly, accept you for who you are!

Smile

The best way to stop being depressed is to stop acting like a depressed person.

Immerse yourself
in great art

Weather patterns

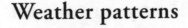

Take a moment to observe the movement of the clouds and the mood of the weather. Consider your own mood – is it a reflection of the weather? At the same time, keep an eye out for any unusual activity in the sky.

Find your purpose

Find a meaningful path in life that reflects your great talents, builds your confidence and protects you from the chaos of emotions.

A visualisation exercise

Allow your body to relax as you picture in your mind a forthcoming task or opportunity. Live through the experience in your imagination before acting on it in real life.

Do a good deed

Get out of your comfort zone and help others less fortunate than yourself.

"The only way to true happiness is to live in the moment and not be worried about the future."

Carrie Bradshaw, *Sex and the City*

Learn to say "No"

Repeat this mantra for self preservation: *I will say "No" when I do not have the time or inclination to act.*

Equine-guided meditation

Imagine you are seeing the world through the horse's eyes, physically and mentally. Imagine how it would feel to have four legs, four hooves and a tail. Establish a connection with these majestic animals for inner peace.

Get a haircut

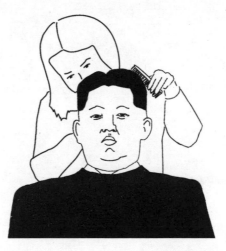

Change your hair – change your life, as Coco
Chanel once said.

Perseverance

Life will always throw challenges our way. Often, all it takes to win the race is an ability to withstand the pressure and persevere despite the losses.

Some calming yoga poses

Here are a few yoga poses for those who have been stuck at their desk for too long. Give them a try – your body and sanity will thank you!

The Torpedo

A great shoulder and upper back stretch for when you are feeling all cramped up.

Hail the Sun King

This may seem like "simply standing", but there is a lot going on.

The Human Shield

An essential pose for building strength and stamina.

The Grenade Pose

A fantastic way to relieve tension.

Keep a journal

De-clutter a frenzied mind by writing your worries down. Seeing them on the page will help bring clarity and perspective.

Togetherness

Surround yourself with like-minded companions
who admire and respect you.

"Happiness is my family;
no matter what's going on."

Kim Kardashian

Don't be afraid of silence...

Sometimes you can achieve more by not saying anything.

Just be aware

Your brain will take care of the rest. And the rest will take care of itself.

A touch of aloe vera

Aloe Vera is that magical plant that just keeps on giving. It is not only good for sunburn, it can kalm down frizzy or dry hair. Comb it through your locks before you blow dry.

Ease back into exercise

It doesn't pay to overdo it.

Communication

Communication is connection, with others and with ourselves, too.

Mindful eating

Focus on your food – which means no multitasking.

Dance

Dancing has been scientifically proven to lower levels of anxiety, stress and depression. Allow yourself a break-out moment everyday to get your groove on.

Spot the goodness in others

Always be observant of those around you.

Interpret your gut

Understand the messages that your body is trying to convey. Is it an omen or just indigestion?

Learn from your stress

The next time you find yourself in what seems like a negative situation, ask yourself this question: Do I have any control over the situation?

"The only thing that people regret is that they didn't live boldly enough... Nothing else really counts at all."

Ted Hughes

Ground yourself

Think of a period of time when you were at your best. Harness these thoughts when you're feeling wobbly.

Savour your surroundings

Give yourself a break from that stress-inducing inner dialogue by being mindful of nature and the earth you walk on – appreciate the soil that brings forth life.

Conserve energy

Only speak when you've got something really good to say.

Give yourself a pat on the back

You are wonderful!

Be part of something bigger than you

Expand your horizons. The world's your oyster!

Listen to your inner voice

Work out your own needs and what makes you feel good.

Find an exercise partner

A work-out shared is a work-out halved. Try these three simple but effective exercises with your gym buddy:

Exercise 1.

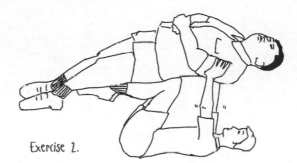

Exercise 2.

Exercise 3.

"You're the only one of you.
Baby, that's the fun of you!"

Taylor Swift

Embody grace

Be graceful in your posture, tone and expressions.
Allow the external to influence the internal.

Self-care

To be compassionate towards others, you must first be compassionate towards yourself.

Learn to turn off your thoughts

Although it's important to listen to your thoughts,
it's equally important to know when to let them go.

Waltz your way to happiness

Waltzing is better for you than working out on a treadmill. Fact. If you are embarrassed about taking formal classes, try it at home alone.

Develop your superpower

Discover your hidden talent – whether it is the art of disguise or the ability to sniff out the truth. Practise and develop these skills, for the benefit of mankind.

A trip to the seaside

Feel the air in your lungs and the wind on your face and let the water calm your mind.

Stay positive

Repeat this mantra: *Everything will work out for me.*

Live life without regrets

Don't dwell on your mistakes. C'est la vie, as the French say. Santé!